21ˢᵗ
Century
Skills Library

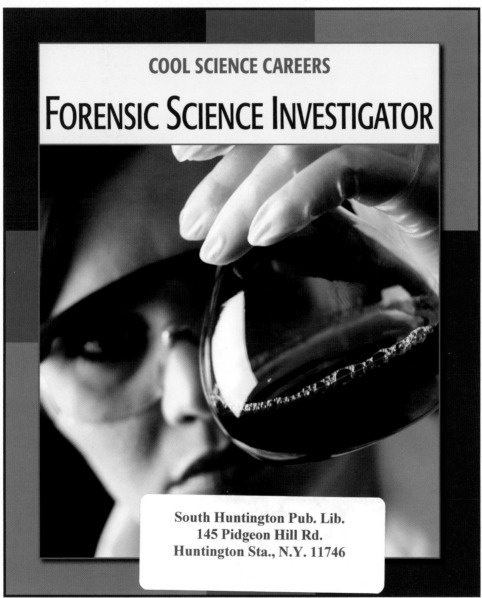

COOL SCIENCE CAREERS

FORENSIC SCIENCE INVESTIGATOR

Tamra Orr

Cherry Lake Publishing
Ann Arbor, Michigan

363.2502
Orr

Published in the United States of America by Cherry Lake Publishing
Ann Arbor, MI
www.cherrylakepublishing.com

Library of Congress Cataloging-in-Publication Data
Orr, Tamra.
  Forensic science investigator / by Tamra Orr.
     p. cm. — (Cool science careers)
  Includes bibliographical references and index.
  ISBN-13: 978-1-60279-055-1 (hardcover : alk. paper)   978-1-60279-081-0 (pbk.)
  ISBN-10: 1-60279-055-8 (hardcover : alk. paper)   1-60279-081-7 (pbk.)
  1. Forensic sciences—Vocational guidance—Juvenile literature. 2.
Forensic scientists—Vocational guidance—Juvenile literature. I. Title.
II. Series.
  HV8073.8.O77 2008
363.25023—dc22   2007005673

Cherry Lake Publishing would like to acknowledge the work of
The Partnership for 21st Century Skills.
Please visit www.21stcenturyskills.org *for more information.*

TABLE OF CONTENTS

CHAPTER ONE

EXPLORING SOME "CRIMES OF THE CENTURY"

Charles and Anne Lindbergh were known around the world after his successful transatlantic flight. Five years later forensics helped solve the kidnapping of their baby.

Crimes of all kinds happen every single day.

What makes people pay more attention to one crime

than another? Often it is that someone involved is

famous. Two cases that have both been called "crimes

of the century" were like this. One occurred in 1932.

The other one came along more than

60 years later. The first one centered on a national

hero, the second on a football star.

Crimes often get sensational coverage by the news media. Think about the news reports of a crime you remember. What was the focus of the reporting? What made it memorable?

The Perfect Life

Charles Lindbergh was a handsome, young, American hero. In 1927, he had become the first person to fly nonstop across the Atlantic Ocean from New York to Paris. Others had tried and failed, so Lindbergh's solo flight electrified people around the world. Soon Lindbergh married Anne Morrow. He taught her to fly an airplane, and they traveled the world together. In 1930, their first child, a boy, was born. Life seemed perfect.

Disaster

Everything was ruined, however, on the cold night of March 1, 1932. At about 9:00 P.M., the 20-month-old baby was kidnapped from the family's home in New Jersey. By 10:30 that night, radio stations across the country were announcing the event. Soon hundreds of tips were coming in to investigators, but none led to the baby.

21st Century Content

Today schools, churches, and community organizations have programs to teach safety from kidnapping. What are some of the most important things to remember about dealing with strangers?

Learning & Innovation Skills

How do you think fame helps some cases to become known as "crimes of the century"? Do you think that whether a victim or suspect is famous or rich should play a part in how a case is treated?

However, a **ransom** note demanding $50,000 had been left in the baby's room. Experts looked at the handwriting on the note. It had been written by someone who had trouble with English grammar and spelling. Other clues were muddy footprints in the nursery and a handmade, wooden ladder leaning against the house. Analysis of the ladder led police to where the wood came from and what kinds of tools made it.

The Lindberghs paid the ransom, but their baby was not returned. The child's body was found in May. However, the ransom money had been "marked." Finally in 1934, the **testimony** of a person who had been paid with the marked ransom money led police to a German

immigrant. His name was Bruno Richard Hauptmann. A search of his

home turned up $14,000 of the ransom. Hauptmann was arrested and

convicted. He was put to death in the electric chair in 1936.

*Today, ransom money is sometimes marked with special
dye to make the money very difficult to use later.*

*O. J. Simpson and Nicole Brown were married
in 1985 and divorced seven years later.*

Evidence Everywhere

The other "crime of the century" began on June 12, 1994. Nicole

Brown Simpson and Ronald Goldman were brutally murdered in front of

Simpson's house in Los Angeles. Evidence included hair, blood, footprints, and a suspicious glove. All the clues pointed to Nicole's former husband, actor and former football star O. J. Simpson. For the next year, Americans everywhere were riveted to their TV sets watching the lengthy trial. More than 800 pieces of evidence were presented.

An Unexpected Verdict

Despite the strong forensic evidence, the final verdict for Simpson was not guilty. Why? Experts believe it was in part because the massive amount of evidence was mishandled. Some was overlooked. Other evidence was **contaminated**. Still other evidence was lost. In the end, the quality of the

investigation and the professionalism of the police officers seemed doubtful. The jury was strongly influenced and found O. J. Simpson not guilty. Many people throughout the nation were shocked!

The Role of Forensic Science

In both of these crimes, forensic science played a huge part. Studying the clues helped lead to the capture and conviction of Bruno Hauptmann in the Lindbergh case in the 1930s. In the 1990s, incorrect handling of the evidence in the Simpson case was a major problem. It became a key factor in the jury's finding of not guilty.

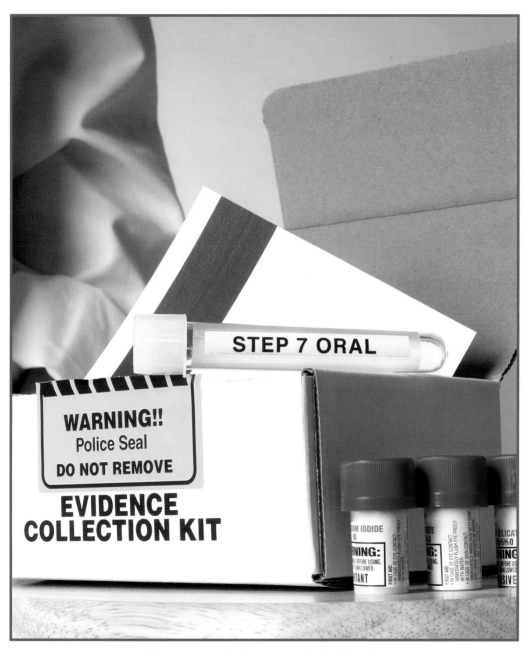

Some companies have created a business by
conveniently packaging evidence tools.

CHAPTER TWO

BEING A FORENSIC SCIENTIST

*Forensic science investigators must carefully look at all the pieces
of evidence and put them together in a logical manner.*

The people who study crime scene clues are known as **forensic**

scientists. They are trained to look at evidence and put it together like a bunch of mismatched puzzle pieces. If all goes well, when they are done, they will have a complete picture of what really happened.

Today's Detectives

Modern-day forensic scientists are all detectives, but they have several different titles and jobs. Two of these types are **pathologists** and **coroners**. A pathologist is a medical doctor who examines human remains to determine the causes and processes of death. A coroner's main duty is to hold an official inquiry into any death by other than natural causes. Sometimes the official inquiry is in front of a jury.

Becoming a pathologist takes many years of schooling. First, you have to graduate from college, and then you have to go to four years of medical school. Then you have to work for several more years in the special area of pathology. Then you must take special written exams. What key personality traits must you have to become a pathologist?

Forensic evidence helped convict Ted Bundy of several murders.

Toxicologists are another kind of forensic scientist. They specialize in

checking for all kinds of chemicals, drugs, gases, and metals in a body's

fluids and tissues. Some dentists are also forensic scientists. They can use

bite marks or dental records to identify a body. In fact, in 1979, a forensic dentist analyzed a bite mark on a murder victim. The analysis led to the capture and conviction of serial killer Ted Bundy. He had murdered 15 people.

All forensic science specialties require many science courses as part of their training. Some of the specialties require a medical degree or other advanced degrees. However, the choice of jobs is broad. Forensic scientists often work for the government. They may also work in private labs or in hospitals and clinics. But no matter where they work, forensic scientists spend most of their time in a lab!

A sign at the chief medical examiner's office in New York City has a saying in Latin. In English it means, "Let conversation cease. Let laughter flee. This is the place where the dead come to aid the living." What does it mean that the dead are helping the living?

A driver's license can provide investigators with a name, address, age, and other key statistics.

Types of Identification

How do forensic scientists identify a victim? They may "get lucky" and find a driver's license or other photo identification such as a credit card. Sometimes family members may be asked to say if they know for sure who it is. Family members may also be able to give a physical description. This could include facts about age, height, and eye color or the type of clothing and jewelry a victim was known to have been wearing.

In other cases, identification is not so easy, so forensic scientists may get medical and dental records. Dental records will list where crowns, fillings, and missing teeth should be. Medical records will describe any tattoos, scars, birthmarks, broken bones, and surgeries. Finally, scientists may request fingerprints. The U.S. military has millions of fingerprints of people who have served. Many employers now require fingerprints, too. Fingerprints are unique because each person's pattern of loops and arches is found on nobody else.

Learning & Innovation Skills

In 1000 A.D., a Roman lawyer named Quintilian used a set of bloody handprints to prove a man was innocent of his mother's murder. How might Quintilian have done this?

CHAPTER THREE

SIFTING THROUGH THE EVIDENCE

The job of a forensic scientist is based on one thing: evidence. It can range from large and obvious to tiny, even **microscopic**. Then it is known as trace evidence.

The most common types of evidence that are analyzed in a lab are hair, DNA, fingerprints, shoe prints, paint, handwriting, dental remains,

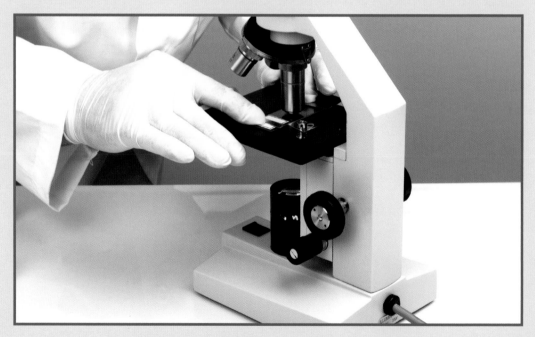

Using a microscope allows investigators to see tiny things that might otherwise have been missed.

stomach contents, and wounds. Other evidence includes bullets, firearms, and other weapons. Also studied will be any blood stains, fibers, bodily fluids, and soil traces.

A Closer Look

Often there are two parts to a forensic scientist's job: to identify and to **individualize**. The first part is often the easiest. For example, it's easy to look at a sample and realize it is dirt. Figuring out exactly what kind of dirt is much trickier. What minerals are in it? Does it contain any seeds? What's the color? When all of this is considered, a scientist might be able to determine exactly where the dirt came from.

Learning & Innovation Skills

French forensic scientist Edmond Locard said, "Every contact leaves a trace." The saying is the basic principle of all forensic science today. What do you think Locard meant?

Into the Courtroom

Forensic scientists are also called on to testify in court about what

they have discovered. They are

considered expert witnesses. To

back up their findings, they often

use photographs, charts, and

diagrams as well as their own

detailed notes and medical reports.

How do they keep track of all of

the pieces of evidence? They put

their initials and the case number

on every piece of physical evidence

with which they come into contact.

The evidence that forensic investigators give in court usually has a strong influence on the jury.

CHAPTER FOUR

TOOLS OF THE TRADE

*Police usually mark off the area of a crime
scene so evidence will not be disturbed.*

Every job has its own special tools that make it easier to do. This is

true for forensic science, too. The tools scientists use on a regular basis

range from the very simple and economical to the extremely complicated

and expensive. You may even have some of the tools in your own house.

However, some of the other tools are highly specialized.

Familiar Equipment

Some of the most important items a forensic scientist uses are quite common. One of these items is a pair of tweezers. The tweezers can pick up small pieces of glass, fiber, or other evidence. Tape is another important tool. It can be used to pick up tiny strands of hair. Other trace evidence can be collected with a vacuum cleaner that has a special filter on it.

Unfamiliar Equipment

One of the most useful pieces of lab equipment is the electron microscope. It greatly magnifies tiny pieces of evidence such as dust mites and **fungal spores**. Other useful lab equipment includes the ultraviolet visible **spectrophotometer**. It can identify

what chemicals a sample contains. Another useful

piece of equipment is the **chromatograph**. It can

analyze drugs. However, all these tools are also very

expensive. Sometimes smaller labs send their samples

to larger, better-equipped labs for analysis.

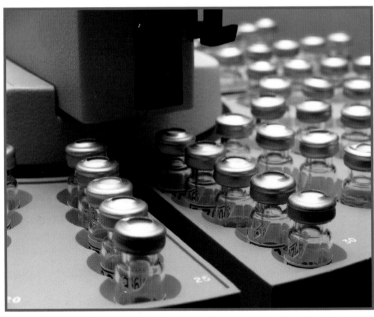

*Investigators can use a gas chromatograph to do
a chemical analysis of a complex substance.*

Today thanks to advances in computers and scientific equipment, law enforcement agencies around the world have access to information collected elsewhere. Interpol, the International Criminal Police Organization, or Scotland Yard, London's police agency, can compare fingerprints or blood samples in the FBI database.

Researchers at places like the Body Farm learn useful facts they can share with forensic investigators worldwide.

Unusual "Equipment"

The University of Tennessee at Knoxville is the home of the

Anthropological Research Facility, better known as the Body Farm. It

began in 1971 with one body on a small plot of land. Now the Body Farm

covers three acres and contains about 40 bodies. Scientists and university

professors study how bodies **decompose** to learn more about forensics.

Every year, workers at the Body Farm hold a memorial service to honor

those whose bodies they use.

CHAPTER FIVE

COPING WITH MASSIVE TRAGEDIES

Forensic scientists have to work even harder than usual when large

tragedies or disasters occur. These types of events have happened many

times throughout history. However, some of the largest have occurred

since the year 2000.

*After the World Trade Center attacks, scientists often
had to use tiny DNA strands to identify victims.*

When many people die at the same time, the task for forensic scientists is huge. They must put together all the clues, help identify the bodies, and determine when and how the victims died.

Thousands of people died in the attacks on the New York World Trade Center and Pentagon, the Indonesia earthquake and tsunami, and Hurricane Katrina. Forensic scientists were overwhelmed with bodies to identify as quickly as possible. DNA was usually their best method, but it is easily damaged by heat and humidity—both of which were present in these events.

Sometimes, even a tiny dust particle like this one can help forensic science investigators better understand a crime.

The first step in solving any crime or dealing with a massive disaster often lies with forensic scientists. It is their job to pull together the many clues, pieces of evidence, and other information to help identify victims and solve crimes. Sadly, until all crime stops and disasters end, the need for forensic scientists will continue.

Glossary

chromatograph (kruh-MAT-uh-graf) machine used to determine chemical components

contaminated (kuhn-TAM-uh-neyt-ed) something made dirty, impure, or polluted

coroner (KOR-uh-ner) one name for an official who investigates suspicious deaths

decompose (dee-kuhm-POHZ) to rot or break down into pieces

forensic scientists (fuh-REN-sik SAHY-uhn-tists) people trained to look at and interpret evidence

fungal spores (FUHNG-guhl spohrz) tiny, one-celled structures in various types of fungus

individualize (in-duh-VIJ-oo-uh-lahyz) to identify down to a single unit

microscopic (mahy-kruh-SKOP-ik) something so small it can only be seen with a microscope

pathologist (puh-THOL-uh-jist) a medical doctor who examines human remains

ransom (RAN-suhm) money demanded for the release of a person or property

spectrophotometer (spek-troh-foh-TOM-i-ter) machine used to measure wavelengths

testimony (TES-tuh-moh-nee) evidence given by a witness, usually in court

toxicologist (tok-si-KOL-uh-jist) expert who looks for the presence of drugs, alcohol, and other elements in body tissues or blood

FOR MORE INFORMATION

Books

Camenson, Blythe. *Opportunities in Forensic Science Careers.*
Chicago: VGM Books, 2001.

Fridell, Ron. *Forensic Science.* Minneapolis: Lerner Publications, 2006.

Jackson, Donna. *The Bone Detectives: How Forensic Anthropologists
Solve Crimes and Uncover Mysteries of the Dead.*
New York: Megan Tingley Books, 2001.

Owen, David. *Police Lab: How Forensic Science Tracks Down
and Convicts Criminals.* Buffalo, NY: Firefly Books, 2002.

Platt, Richard. *Forensics.* New York: Kingfisher Books, 2005.

Twist, Clint. *The Great Forensic Challenge.*
Hauppauge, NY: Barron's, 2005.

Other Media

http://library.thinkquest.org/04oct/00206/index1.htm is a
good website to find out more about what forensic scientists do.

www.aafs.org is the website of the professional
association to which many forensic scientists belong.

History's Mysteries "Buried Secrets: Digging for DNA."
DVD. The History Channel.

Modern Marvels "Forensic Science: The Crime-Fighter's Weapon."
DVD. The History Channel.

INDEX

ABOUT THE AUTHOR

Tamra Orr is a full-time writer and author living in the gorgeous Pacific Northwest. She loves her job because she learns more about the world every single day and then turns that information into pop quizzes for her patient and tolerant children (ages 16, 13, and 10). She has written more than 80 nonfiction books for people of all ages, so she never runs out of material and is sure she'd be a champion on *Jeopardy*.